The Trinidad Carnival:

Not Just Carnival in Trinidad

Clyde A. Weatherhead

i

The Trinidad Carnival:
Not Just Carnival in Trinidad

© 2019 Clyde A. Weatherhead

Cover photo – Esau Millington, Midnight Robber, playing mas at age 94 – Photo by the Author

OTHER PUBLICATIONS BY THE AUTHOR

Speaking Out: A Collection of Letters and Other Writings - 1991 – 1993, 2018 (paperback and kindle editions)

The Future of Mas: Children of the Carnival (Images from the Children's Carnival 2006 (kindle edition)

Available on Amazon

Dedicated to Esau Millington and all the mas makers and players, the Creators of the Steelpan, the Players of instruments, the Singers and Kaisonians.

For all the guardians of The Trinidad Carnival past, present and yet to come, who have and continue to keep its Spirit Alive.

Contents

Acknowledgements

To my father, Clyde O., artist, mas-maker and -player for inducting me into The Trinidad Carnival.

To my life-long friend, Brian Honore' with whom I played mas in primary school and shared so many cultural moments in and out of the Carnival.

To the pannists of Turban Starland, Tunapuna All Stars, Voices, Humming Birds Pan Groove and Curepe Sforzata with whom I shared the road and Panorama stage.

To my comrades of the People's Cultural Association with whom I had the honour of performing and creating mas for the youth of the 1980's.

To Russel 'Slim' Andalcio who was pivotal in the **Students For Change** publication featured in this book and which contributed to the debate on The Trinidad Carnival and the culture of the people of our beloved Trinbago.

To Anthony 'Melloncolly' Collymore and companeros who keep the Mystery Raiders banner waving on the city streets in tribute to our founder - Brian 'O'Cangaceiro' Honore', Andrew 'Puggy' Joseph, Esau 'Midnight Killer' Millington and Charles 'King Oleander' Harington – lifelong mas players who inspire us.

To all who have walked the road on Carnival day so we and those to come continue to do so.

Author's Preface

This book is about the phenomenon proclaimed the Greatest Show on Earth – **The Trinidad Carnival.**

In it, are three essays written between 1976 and 2006 by the Author, as part of a collective or as individual, forming part of an analysis of the phenomenon that is The Trinidad Carnival.

This analysis has developed out of my participation in various aspects of The Carnival at various stages of his life.

From as early as the age of three, growing up a few houses away from the Eastern Main Road in Tunapuna, the main venue of the town's Carnival activities, as a spectator, I saw the mas and the mass participation in the ritual of the Carnival.

Mr. Brown who lived higher up Hackett Lane transformed into the Midnight Robber for two days of The Carnival. A man we all knew became the character we feared.

Over the years, trekking to the bleachers just past the big stage at the Queen's Park Savannah, my siblings and I in tow with my grandmother and mother, our pleasant task was to provide the sustenance to my father – the red Indian, crusading knight, African warrior, devilish imp – or whatever character he assumed as a mas man in Saldenah's band.

Our house and yard were the mas camp for him and his friends from BWIA and Chetwyn's Tennis Club who made and played their mas together for many years.

In that mas camp, I learned many titbits of the art of making mas.

My father also made my first mas costume when I became a musketeer playing mas at primary school and my brother, the jolly green giant.

Those Carnival art skills were most useful when later, I was involved in the production of a children's carnival band produced by the Children's Workshop, which organised camps in various communities during the long August vacation.

The children learnt about The Carnival and the next Carnival's portrayals at the camp. They learnt the significance of the mas they would be playing and even the dances.

One year we played sailor mas. Three hundred plus children on the streets of Port of Spain on Carnival Saturday.

Seven months earlier on the streets of Maloney, La Horquetta, Chaguanas, Diego Martin and San Fernando these sailors danced the sailor dance in preparation.

I was again to play mas when I joined the Mystery Raiders on the streets of Port of Spain, playing Robber mas in salute to Brian Honore, the founder of the Mystery Raiders and my mas playing companion in Primary School and fellow participant in the culture and The Carnival in many ways since.

I have played pan with Turban Starland and Tunapuna All Stars on the Eastern Main Road on which I was introduced to the Carnival as a child.

More recently, I have assisted in the production of children's mas when my daughter played with the children of the Princess Elizabeth Centre for several years.

I also have been photographing the children's mas, the future of the mas, and writing about The Carnival.

I continue to go to the Mystery Raiders mas camp to help with making the mas despite my physical challenges preventing my playing the mas.

This thing – The Trinidad Carnival – once you get involved with it, it does not let you go.

I am eternally grateful to my father for putting me in touch with The Carnival.

Happily, The Carnival is in me. It is in all ah we.

The Trinidad Carnival is at the heart of the Trinbago culture.

We must never let it become just another carnival.

Clyde A. Weatherhead

February 2019

Introduction

Like all things in nature, the Trinidad Carnival is shaped by its duality, the unity and struggle of two opposite tendencies that are its roots and content.

This Carnival was born of a clash of two cultures in the firmament of the reclamation of their humanity in the culture of the ex-slaves at Emancipation and the cultural influence of the plantocracy.

Ever since, there have been opposing definitions of the Carnival in submerged and sometime open battle to define, shape and determine the future of The Trinidad Carnival.

This 2-root essence finds expression in the contemporary 'bikini-and-beads' and 'traditional' trends in the mas.

Particularly, since the cultural renaissance of the 1970 Revolution, this struggle of opposing tendencies has been recognised and analysed more deeply in understanding the history and uniqueness of The Trinidad Carnival.

It is not just another carnival. It is The Carnival.

The article "Recapture the True Spirit of Carnival" published by the Students For Change organisation in 1976 was an important contribution to this understanding of the Trinidad Carnival.

The development of The Carnival has been described over the years as the movement from Masquerade to Carnival.

The Trinidad Carnival

From the masked balls of the plantation aristocracy to the street mas and theatre of the former slaves and working people to merely 'playing mas' or the 'biggest street party' as those who attempt to re-assert the dominance of the 'frivolity of the plantation house balls' on the Carnival.

This struggle between the Kamboulay and the Mardi Gras continues to rage today in the core of The Carnival.

Whether it is in the mas, the Calypso-Soca or Steelpan arenas which are all integral parts of the Trinidad Carnival, this battle for the heart of The Carnival continues.

An interview with a veteran mas-man now mas tutor published in 2013 put it this way:
"People hardly play individual mas. ...... Carnival people have abandoned the individual mas. They want to see a naked mas on stage. But Carnival is not that, it is no "Mickey Mouse" thing. Play a little Indian mas here, a little Robber mas there. ... This is mas! ... people and them fed up with the naked mas. Every year, one kind of thing. Beads and a panty and bra!".

Titles on The Carnival from Dr. Hollis Liverpool's "Rituals of Power & Rebellion" to Jeff Henry's "Under the Mas': Resistance and Rebellion in the Trinidad Masquerade" to a recent "The Business of Bacchanal: how can Trinidad and Tobago develop its Carnival Industry as a viable export product and developmental tool ?" point to the ongoing battle for the heart and soul of The Carnival.

In 2019, the debate on The Carnival; What it is, What it is for, Where it needs to go − this debate has reached the point of attempts to re-define The Carnival.

One commentator recently said that our Carnival is unique because "it is not about the 2 days anymore. It is about a season of parties, an experience for the visitors".

The striving for the tourist dollar, the obsession with building marketing 'networks' to make our music international these are not new to The Carnival.

This commercialising has had expression in the conversion of mas making into the contemporary showcase-imported costumes-masquerade.

The superficial, commercialised, over-competitive direction that is being promoted is the direction of converting The Trinidad Carnival into just another carnival in Trinidad.

The defence of The Trinidad Carnival demands that its history be understood and preserved.

It demands that unique and indigenous qualities of the Kamboulay root of The Carnival must be preserved and given modern form and expression.

The preservation of The Trinidad Carnival is part of the resistance to the indistinguishable culture that denies national character that is called 'world' culture or global culture that threatens national identity in the service of a world resembling the old order at the time of the Emancipation.

RECAPTURE THE TRUE SPIRIT OF CARNIVAL

First Published in
STUDENTS FOR CHANGE
Vol. No.1 March-April 1976

This article is merely a glance, a peep into the rich and glorious Cultural traditions of our People. It is intended to serve as the beginning of a series of articles analysing the rich Cultural history of our People. It is hoped that this series will serve to urge genuine anti-Imperialist artistes and cultural workers to contribute to the investigation and analysis of our Cultural history, and to work towards consciously developing the genuine anti-Imperialist People's Culture of Trinago.

THE BEGININGS

Carnival started in Trinidad, in the days before slavery was abolished, as a celebration of the French slave owning planter class. It was originally a festival of the ruling classes only. At that time the class division of the society was easily observable.

The representatives of the Colonizers who manned the State machinery were Europeans; the very big Planters were white West-Indians; the small peasant farmers, the "middle class" petty traders, etc. were "free men of colour".

The labouring masses were by vast majority African Slaves, and few Amerindians. In the period prior to the emancipation of Slavery in 1834, the upper classes celebrated the Carnival free from any restrictions.

There existed however restrictions controlling the "free men of colour", as summed up by L.M. Fraser, the Chief of Police in Trinidad, in a memorandum to the Governor in 1881 following the Canboulay Riots:

> *In former days down to the period of the emancipation of the slaves the Carnival was kept up with much spirit by the upper classes. There are many persons still living who remember the masked balls given at St. Anns by the Governor, Sir Ralf Woodford . . . and also that the leading members of society used on the days of Carnival to drive through the streets of Port of Spain masked, and in the evenings go from house to house which were all thrown open for the occasion.*
>
> *The Free Men of colour were subjected to very stringent regulations and although not forbidden to mask, were yet compelled to keep to themselves and never to join in the amusement of the privileged classes..."*

Slave revolts were common during Carnival season. In fact, the entire period of African Slavery in the Caribbean is characterised by constant slave rebellions. So common were the slave revolts during the period from Christmas to Ash Wednesday that:

> " . . . *To forestall such attempts it became a practice in the British Colonies to proclaim Martial Law over the Christmas and New Year holidays. On December 24th, each year, guns were fired from the Forts on the island, a red flag was hoisted, civil tribunals were suspended and military law was enforced. The entire militia was on duty, and business literally came to a halt. There were troop parades and mock engagements...*"
> (from Errol Hill, Trinidad Carnival)

August 1st 1834 was Emancipation Day, but the Carnival of 1834 was already taken over by the working class of ex-slaves.

The mas players ridiculed the Colonial masters, they mocked, mimicked and satirized the actions of the Armed Forces in their military parades.

The first mas band of this type was seen in 1834; it was known as the Artillery Band.

This mas was so effective that in the *Port-of-Spain Gazette* of the 14th February 1834, the Editor wrote: *"the mockery of the best Militia Band that has been embodied in the West was in very bad taste . . ."*

After emancipation these military mas bands developed, and it was around these bands that Working-Class Carnival developed.

CANBOULAY

The ex-slaves celebrated emancipation on August 1st of every year, in a form that became known as Canboulay.

The form of the celebration was similar to the forced march of slaves from Plantation Barracks to the scene of a big Cane Fire (Cannes Brullees means Burnt Cane).

In the same memorandum to the Governor in 1881, the Chief of Police wrote of Cannes Brullees:

"In the days of slavery whenever a fire broke out upon an estate the slaves on the surrounding properties were immediately mustered and marched to the spot, horns and shells were blown to collect them and the gangs were followed by the drivers cracking their whips and urging with cries and blows to their work.

After emancipation the negroes began to represent this scene as a kind of commemoration of the change in their condition, and the procession of the cannes brulees' used to take place on the night of the 1st August, the date of emancipation. . . . After a time the day was changed and for many years past the Carnival days have been inaugurated by the ' Cannes Brulees'.

During the early days of slavery, the plantation slaves were legally permitted to carry long sticks, to protect themselves from snakes and to use as a tool to assist in cutting cane. These sticks became, in the hands of the slaves a dangerous weapon.

Over the years the art of warfare using sticks was developed and perfected. Eventually slaves were prohibited from carrying sticks in 1810.

During Canboulay the ex-slaves marched with sticks (bois).

The whipping of the slaves during the forced march to the cane fires was hatefully remembered and during the Canboulay the idea of slavery was symbolized by the Jab Mollassi (Molasses Devil). This character was played by a man who covered his entire skin with a mixture of soot (symbolic of the cane ashes) and molasses (from the sugar factories).

The molasses devil was beaten with whips during the solemn procession.

Freedom songs were sung, and songs used just before and during a slave revolt were recalled and sung; stick-fighting contests would take place.

THIS CELEBRATION DROVE FEAR INTO THE HEARTS OF THE RULING CLASSES.

As to exactly how and when Canboulay and Carnival celebrations became joined into one is not known. However, it is known that Canboulay and stick-fighting dominated Carnival until 1884 when Canboulay was banned and stick-fighting severely restricted by law.

Carnival became a FESTIVAL OF PROTEST of the masses. FROM THE TIME THE CHARACTER OF CARNIVAL CHANGED FROM THE FRIVOLOUS GAIETY OF THE UPPER CLASSES TO THE FESTIVAL OF PROTEST OF THE MASSES OF OPPRESSED PEOPLE; THE LOCAL UPPER CLASSES AND THEIR COLONIAL MASTERS TRIED TO STOP CARNIVAL.

In 1846 the Governor banned the wearing of masks. There was serious rioting in Port-of-Spain.

In 1858 and again in 1859 the Police were sent to stop Carnival. The entire Police Force was beaten by stick fighters and it was the troops with heavier arms that temporarily stopped the Carnival.

In San Fernando in 1871 and 1872, the Police tried to stop this Carnival Festival of Protest. This attempt led to serious fights between the Police and the People.

In 1881 the Canboulay riots took place. This was the most serious clash between the Police and the People.

The battle waged for the right to protest was so intense that from that time onwards, up till very recently, British Battleships were sent to Trinidad and stood in readiness in the Port-of-Spain Harbour.

As a protest against the presence of Naval troops in the Harbour, "Sailor mas" developed and the British sailors were depicted as drunken fools. 64The dance of the "drunken sailor" developed out of the mas ridiculing the British Navy.

In 1884, 3 people were killed in Princess Town as people fought for the right to hold the Festival of Protest. In that same year, 1884, the famous Hosein Riots took place in South Trinidad.

The ban imposed on the use of the skin drum led to the development of a new musical form in Trinidad, the Tambour Bamboo. Later in the 1930's the Tambour Bamboo gave way to a new form that emerged with the growth and development of the Oil Industry - the Steel band.

ARTISTIC EXPRESSIONS OF MILITANCY SUPPRESSED

As Carnival developed, Stickfight Bands led by Shantwells (singers) developed. The Shantwells would compose and sing "war" songs, praising the skill of his fighters, recounting many historic battles fought and won and he predicting nothing but a horrible death of his opponents.

After 1884, with the banning of the Stick fight Bands, the shantwell bandleader gradually phased out. Eventually the restrictions on the stickfighters became so fierce that stick fight lost its true meaning.

Today the ruling puppets of American Imperialism have made efforts to re-introduce the stick fight in their "Better Village" competitions and in their Dimanche Gras Show. This is because of the Sale Value of stickfight to tourists who regards stickfight as a dance of "quaint savagery".

With the decline of stickfight Bands, individual fighters dressed as Pierrots (clowns) took to the streets on Carnival Days, These Pierrots were originally the playful clowns of the ruling classes. Taken over by the masses, Pierrots were given a new character. In his book, 'Trinidad Carnival', Errol Hill notes that: "*The Pierrot is a traditional European carnival character whose disguise was popular with the propertied classes of the pre-emancipation era...*""

From the prankish witty but harmless, European clown, the Pierrot in Trinidad became a loquacious, combative and fearless masker whose rhetorical skill was merely a prelude to violent duel with whips and sticks."

In order to control the Pierrots, the Governor ordered that they must register with the Police from 1892 onwards. The anonymity of the mas was wiped out. And the very idea of registering with the Police to play mas was repulsive. The Pierrot mas was effectively suppressed and by 1920 very few players played the Pierrot.

Today in the countryside, and particularly in Princess Town, the Pierrot has survived but the players are old men. The combative spirit is, however, still present.

During the "Don't Cut" Campaign of the Cane Farmers in 1975, one Pierrot was heard referring to his opponents as Girwar's[1] representatives. This Pierrot boasted of having killed many Girwar-men and of routing the entire Police Force who came to the protection of Girwar.

On investigation he was found to be an old Cane Cutter from the Valley Line in Barrackpore[2].

The true spirit of Carnival still exists in pockets of the countryside, in areas far away from the overbearing influence of the American Imperialists and their puppet organised competitions.

FROM MAS TENTS TO ASSEMBLY LINES

The first mas band that appeared in 1834 was a Military mas band. Military mas remained the mas of the Working Class until 1971 when all military mas was banned by the Government.

It was around the Military band that mas tents developed. Originally the bands put on Pantomime plays ridiculing the armed forces. Later on, these

---

[1] After Norman Girwar, the Manager of TICFA, the Association hated by the very small farmers of the Southern countryside
[2] Barrackpore was the centre of the Cane farmers Struggle in 1974 and 1975

plays conveyed ideas of protest, and were led by singing shantwells.

The mas tent became a People's Theatre in the backyards of the working-class districts. At that time (and still today to a lesser extent) the workers in the towns lived in huddled settlements, in barracks crowded around an open yard. It was these barrack yards that were converted into Theatres during the Carnival Season.

These backyard Theatres were known as tents. In these tents costumes were made, the pantomime was decided upon and rehearsed, musicians would play, and the shantwells would introduce their new songs, which the people would learn. These songs involved answering chants from the people. There would also be stickfights and dancing.

Over the years with the development of Capitalism and the devious means by the Colonial masters to suppress the People's Theatres, the very character of the mas tents changed.

Eventually, Calypso tents developed separate from mas tents where only costumes were produced.

These mas tents developed into artistic workshops. Costumes were made with the emphasis on meticulous detail.

Historical mas developed and "masmen" bandleaders would study the history of the periods or events which they wished to portray.

Masmen prided themselves in their knowledge of history and in their ability to recapture exactly the clothing used during the period portrayed.

A viking was a viking with real leather, goatskin, etc. A roman soldier was a roman soldier; complete with chest plate, shield, shin guards, etc.; all with fantastic metal working of intricate designs.

Carnival became a phenomenal display of artistic creations, with real-life historical events portrayed.

The real mas players were the masses, with thousands of soldiers, Sailors, with Tanks, Battleships, Bazookas, Armoured Cars, etc., Red Indians with beautifully designed headpieces, and also historical mas portrayals. The middle and upper classes played "social mas".

We have been the victims of a giant conspiracy.

The ruling Classes unable to crush the Carnival Festival of Protest, set up the machinery to control Carnival through their repressive Laws, their Battleships and armed forces.

They then set up elaborate machinery to organise the competitions. THEY APPOINT JUDGES. THEY DECIDE UPON CATEGORIES. THEY USE THEIR NEWSPAPERS TO PROPAGANDIZE THE TYPE OF MAS THAT IS "GOOD".

Today the whole emphasis has been shifted with all kinds of airy-fairy mas pushed as <u>real</u> mas. <u>This is inevitable for so long as the Competitions remain the centre of Carnival.</u>

It is the Upper Classes that set the standards for judging these competitions. Since they control the competitions, the definition of 'real mas' has been changed.

As a result, today "good mas" is all kinds of airy-fairy artistry, Meaningless abstract, ideas-mas; silky, flimsy, see-through, breezy, substance-less portrayals reflecting the superficial shallowness and falseness of bourgeois creators and promoted in the press as 'good mas'.

Whenever, the masses are shown in their magazines and newspapers, it is either drunk on a pavement sleeping in vomit, or the bottom of a young woman in a tight pants.

As a result, the 'winners' are always the bands controlled by Berkley, Lee Heung, Hart, etc.

These bands are produced in Factories, run on a Capitalist basis. Even the designer of the "Winners' Band" is an employee. All the people making mas are workers employed by the bandleader.

The leader sells them the "right" to play mas and the costume to play it in. The Capitalist mode of production has taken over the "successful" bands.

Many of the shoes worn by mas players this year as part of their costume, were produced by a shoe-manufacturing Factory at the Diamond-Vale Industrial Estate, in Diego Martin.

Today the Carnival of the Savannah Competition and the Dimanche Gras shows, Is the Carnival of the Capitalists.

CALYPSO - PROTEST OR OBSCENE FRIVOLITY?

The shantwell leaders of the stickfight bands became the calypsonians. In many ways this is an oversimplification. The development of calypso as a musical and poetic form has its origins in peasant and Tribal cultural forms.

In Venezuela among the people of Amerindian descent there was a type of topical song known as CARISO.

It is felt that the musical form of calypso is influenced strongly by a Venezuelan-Amerindian dance tune known as PASEO.

West African topical songs known as WUSO also were known in the Caribbean.

It is recorded by Bryan Edwards, an 18th century historian, in "The History, Civil and Commercial, of the British Colonies" that the slaves sang songs of a calypso type:

"At the merry meetings and midnight festivals they are not without ballads of

another kind, adapted for such occasions, and here they give full scope to a talent for ridicule, which is exercised not only against each other but also not infrequently, at the expense of their owner or employer . . . "

The following is recorded in the "Journal of a West India Proprietor" by Matthew Lewis, a slave owner of Jamaica. This song was sung by the leader of a slave revolt, "the king of the Eboes", during the preparations for the revolt.

Oh me good friend, Mr. Wilberforce, make we free!

God Almighty thank ye! God.

Almighty thank ye!

God Almighty make we free!

Bukra in this country, no make we free:

What Negro for to do? What Negro for to do?

Take force by force! Take force by force!

Chorus

To be sure! To be sure!

To be sure!

In 1899, the editorial of the *Port-of-Spain Gazette* refers to calypso singing and the original mas tents:

"There are various bands of these roughs which have been organised for the coming carnival (and who) congregate, we understand, for the practising of ribald songs which axe to be sung during the two days of the fete. These songs axe for the most part intended to bring certain persons into ridicule..."

The first known calypso in English is critical of the Governor Jerningham, for is interference in the affairs of the Port-of-Spain City Council. It was sung in 1898:

Jerningham the Governor

Is a fastness in to you

Is a rudeness in to you

To break up the laws of

The Borough Council

The essence of Calypso is PROTEST. The calypsonian has always been the spokesman for the sentiments of the oppressed.

Following the strike of the dockworkers in 1919, the calypsonian "Chinese Patrick" sang:

Class legislation is the order of this land

We are ruled with the iron hand

During the famous strike of the oil workers in South Trinidad in 1937, a "strikers calypso" was sung; some of the lyrics were as follows:

We workers is so many

Working for de oil company

We strike in Point an' Fyzabad

Against the oil robbers of Trinidad . . .

Up till at least 1960, this striker's calypso was sung by Jab Molassi in Fyzabad.

On the campus at U.W.I. St. Augustine, the Calypso King for 1970, the Mindbender, sang:

If anyone feel it ain't go have war in dis country

Is either he deaf, he drunk or he dam stupidy ...

A great transformation took place in calypso as a direct result of the occupation of Trinidad by American Imperialist soldiers during the war of 1939-1945. The Capitalist-minded tent managers, saw money making possibilities in the presence of Yankee soldiers roaming the streets of the city in search of entertainment, with their pockets filled with Yankee dollars.

The hardship of the war years, the constant shortages and rationing, the shortage of money and employment, led to the birth and the rapid growth of prostitution in the cities. The daughters and wives of poor workers were driven by economic hardship to prostitute themselves to American soldiers.

The East Dry River area, in Port-of-Spain and the village of Carenage became the hunting grounds for Yankee soldiers. The urban men hated the soldiers and there were many violent clashes between the young men of the city and the yankee soldiers.

The naked and vicious rape of our urban womanhood was the price extracted from our country for the presence of American Imperialist Troops.

Some of the calypso tents became the dens of obscene vulgarity as singers prostituted themselves and their art to the decadence of the American soldiers.

A struggle developed between the Old Brigade calypsonians, striving to retain the old Kaiso; and the Young Brigade calypsonians, offering their art for sale to the Americans by catering more and more to the tastes of the Americans.

Smut and all forms of vulgar frivolity took over these tents as nightclub type entertainment was provided for the Yankee.

More or less, the Young Brigade won out and the calypso as we know it today, resulted. However, there are calypsonians who have resisted the decadence and who have kept Old Brigade-type calypso alive.

The extent of the control of the media over the values and ideas of our people is demonstrated by the fact that the calypsonian who sings protests songs today is regarded as a rebel.

TOURIST FESTIVAL

Because of their control of the machinery of the State, the ruling Classes have been able to suppress those aspects of Carnival which served the interests of the Masses of the people; with the aid of their laws[3] and the threat and use of armed force.

With their newspapers, radio and television and through the financing of competitions they have promoted the carnival that serves the interests of the Hotel owners, Food and Drink manufacturers, and the mas-factory owners posing as Band Leaders.

They have shaped and molded a new carnival to cater to the tastes of the tourists. The Police and the Courts were given special Carnival instructions to protect the Tourists In 1976.

All carnival pictures in Tourist Brochure& and magazines show flimsily clad women, dancing with legs exposed, belly exposed, breasts exposed; wining and gyrating.

---

[3] *Steelbands had to apply to the Police for permits "to play pans and beat drums" so that they could play music on Carnival days.*

Carnival advertisements promote the idea of brown skinned girls, barely clothed and laughing invitingly at Tourists.

Trinidad is promoted as a country of fun; of happy-go-lucky people.

Massive banners stream across all the main roads advertising FREE CONTRACEPTIVES FOR CARNIVAL. Sex and carnival are promoted and made into synonyms as these carnival banners warn against CARNIVAL BABIES.

Male and female prostitution is openly advertised.

Calypsoes tell "Miss Tourist" about the power of the "Iron Man". Calypsoes telling about a "bum--bum!' carnival; "saltfish"; and "Tut-Tuts"; are promoted by the radio stations.

This year Sparrow's "Jamming" was promoted, and the Jamming dance was promoted as THE dance for '76. As a result of the tremendous influence of the advertising machine of the Capitalists, mas players told to jam one another In front or behind, were doing just that in order to be "with it".

RECAPTURE THE SPIRIT OF CARNIVAL

Today the masses of the people are being driven away from carnival. Bands which formerly fielded thousands of people in the great military mas of the times, now struggle to draw together a couple hundred.

There are however a few protest bands. However, the form of these band's presentations needs serious development in the area of artistic work.

It is the responsibility of all serious artistes and all lovers of genuine carnival, to come together and recreate the Theatre of the streets.

Let us reject the C.D.C. operated Tourist Festival of the Stages.

Let us turn our backs on the Capitalists' carnival.

Playwriters must come forward and use their skills to serve the people, by presenting plays on the streets reflecting the sentiments of the oppressed. Calypso tents must live once more to reflect the sentiments of the oppressed, not to draw out vulgar guffaws from tourists.

IT IS OUR RESPONSIBILITY AND OUR DUTY TO RECAPTURE THE TRUE SPIRIT OF CARNIVAL.

LET US INVESTIGATE THE HISTORY AND CULTURE OF OUR PEOPLE!

CARNIVAL MENTALITY

From *Speaking Out:*
A Collection of Letters and Other Writings
First Published 1993

Some of the most interesting things in life come to us by surprise. In the heat of the dry season afternoon, the prospect of any pleasantries in the midst of the miles of highway traffic seemed remote.

But, by chance the journey from Port of Spain to Maloney with my chance passenger turned out to be one that covered some forty years of history yesterday afternoon.

What he told me about the history and development of our Carnival and Steelband was so refreshing that the heat and carbon monoxide seemed to disappear.

I hope that discussions, as we had, can be held to really dispel what I consider the foul attempt to discredit our rich cultural heritage that is Carnival. And, along with this the clouds of pious bigotry that are looming to divide our people even on this must also be dispelled.

Just last Saturday, there was another discussion on Carnival and Steelband. Like the declarations of clerics of the Muslim and Hindu faiths recently, the secular experts came to the same amazing conclusion - Carnival is devil-worship. Either stay away or rally the forces of goodness to fight this evil.

Well if they listened to the stories of my passenger who took me through the journey from tamboo bamboo to biscuit tin bass to the bass skittle and the do-doop, right up to the evolution of the higher tone pans which could not play "a whole tune", they might be better off.

My friend also talked about how the chantuelle and the lavway were replaced by the "sweet music" and how Paul Anika singing "Diana" became the Road March King one year.

We talked about brass band and the hall bass, how brass and drum used to be so nice together. We talked about the old brigade and the young brigade and which male calypsonian introduced "man wining on stage" and win crown in 1992.

We talked about how chipping was not a las' lap thing, but, the real action to the steelband music and how that sound in the evening compelled you to join the band.

We also talked about wine and jock waist. Because, before that calypsonian start wining on stage for the Yankees, only women and homosexuals used to wine on the street. Men used to do the jock waist, really a take-off from the bongo dance and "it didn't have no wine in dat".

And, then we talked about the nakedness. My friend so wisely responded, "That is only commercial. The bandleader want to sell a costume to make money.

So, if he used to give you a tights and a bathsuit, now he will give you a bathsuit alone. And, if you cut off piece of the bathsuit, it cost him less and your bottom outside."

Finally, the dreaded "D" word. "You mean they doh know that Carnival start off as a celebration of freedom", he pointed out. "Is only the colonial master tell the people that carnival bad and after they must go for ashes. You remember they used to say you can't sing calypso in lent. Now the priest playing mas, so you have calypso right through".

Well, I thought, how wise. This man who lived through the days of the last five decades, who remembers J'ouvert starting at midnight and is mas right through to Tuesday night. This man lived to see sadly "modern" mas resting Monday night so they could go in the competition Tuesday.

Who was I to doubt a man who was around Zigilee, the bass skittle master, who heard Spree play a whole tune for the first time and it was a hymn, when he said "Carnival is we culture!". His honesty piety led him to conclude "the slaves praised God for their freedom and called the old slave master the White Devil". That is Carnival.

Well, I hope that somebody gets the message. Stop trying to degrade our very rich and uplifting cultural expressions. Stop trying to take away the blame from the money men who have corrupted the Carnival to fatten their pockets. Stop trying to blame the people for the promotion of vulgarity which was introduced when Jean and Dinah were forced to work for the Yankee dollar.

Trinidad Carnival is unique. It is the development of the Canboulay in which the Molasses Devil (Jab Molassi) was the target of ridicule and hatred as a symbol of the slavery that had ended.

In today's Carnival those who see only the corruption of this fine tradition by those who are only interested in money and selling our Carnival to some tourist market, must be half blind.

They don't see, like my wise friend, that there is a strong trend in the opposite direction - seeking to bring back the real spirit and traditions of We Carnival. "Just imagine" he said, "I heard a band coming up the road Monday and it sounded like the old steelband and I say how them fellas know to play that so".

Well it's just that the old, really beautiful things of our traditional past are still with us. Just look at the fact that there was bamboo back in the pan round de neck this year, devil mas and JAB was road march. In the Children's mas the old-time characters coming back stronger all the time, in new fashion. Even the singers had to start talking about long time band and jock yuh waist and wine. Who knows soon they may be going back to wine and jock waist like before.

Carnival is not to be used for telling people to despise their own culture. It is not an occasion to try and put people against one another by appealing to religious rectitude and super morality.

The festival of freedom and protest against the evils in the society must be returned to that status. Let the world really marvel at the wonder of the true Trini Carnival. Let us not sell ourselves short.

Thanks, Landeau.

1992:March:17

Talk! Robber Man

Remembering Brian Honore'

aka

O'Cangaceiro

Commentor

Sir B

February 2006

A People's Cultural Association Publication

About the Publishers

The **People's Cultural Association (PCA)** *is an association of progressive artistes and cultural workers dedicated to serving the people's interests on the front of art and culture. The PCA has taken up the task of preserving and developing the progressive and democratic traditions of our people and to advancing cultural resistance to all forms of decadent and divisive culture, foreign or local.*

The PCA encourages all artistes to use what is best in the traditions of our people's culture to promote the unity of the people arid to support their struggles for the advance of society, for independence and sovereign rights and for freedom.

Dedication and Acknowledgements

The People's Cultural Association extends its deepest gratitude to all those who supported the work to make this publication a reality. Special thanks to those who offered comments and suggestions and contributed material.

In particular, to Ms. Eileen Honore who has been a source of inspiration, to Anthony 'Melloncolly Marauder' Collymore for supplying several photographs, to the members and supporters of the association who have in various ways ensured that we pay fitting tribute to someone who contributed tremendously to our work over many years and to our people's culture in the hope that this will encourage many others to follow in the footsteps of the person whose example we seek to record.

This book is dedicated to the memory of Brian Honore', to the recognition of his outstanding contribution and to the people to whose cause he devoted his entire life and his talents. This book is also dedicated to the many contributors to the people's culture of resistance including Andrew 'Puggy' Joseph, Esau Millington and all those artistes who today are making their contributions.

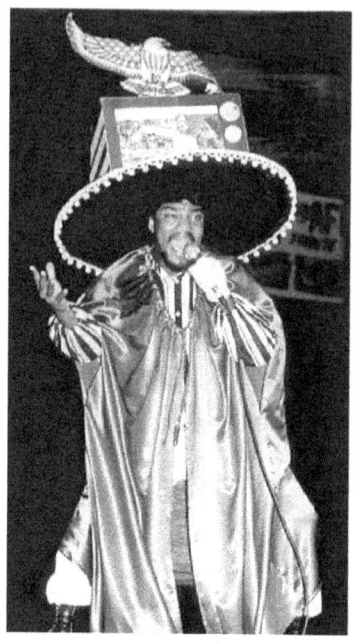

Brian Anthony Honore'
O'Cangaceiro
21 July 1955 – 17 May

Talk Robber Man

Into the glare of the setting sun rode the badman of the Brazilian sertao ... the Reincarnation of O'Cangaceiro. Surrounded by companeros from far and wide across the landscape of the Mas land....he rode for the last time.

He had left his mark. Eighteen and more years terrorising the playgrounds of desolation and destruction...he fought the notorious and the profane.

May 23[1]2005 was the last ride of Brian Anthony Honore, aka Sir B, Commentor, O'Cangaceiro, Robber Man, or sundry other sobriquets depending on the stage or stages of his life at which you made his acquaintance.

He took his last ride along Main Street in the country-town (as one writer describes it) of Tunapuna, the place from whence he came.

This place has been the crucible of many an icon of our people in politics, sport, culture and every facet of social life.

The Beginnings

A baby is not born in a vacuum. He is born into the womb of history dripping with all its nourishment and poisons as well.

Brian's love for culture must have had its roots in the nurturing of Eileen Honore', affectionately called 'Ms. Hons' by all his friends.

She is herself a woman of a sense of culture and dignity. She punctuates any conversation with liberal sprinklings from the literary classics.

Brian must have been a son in whom she is well pleased.

As with the children of many public servants of that time, Brian's education shifted wherever his mother was moved as a teacher.

In this case, the move was into the capital city.

The latter years of his primary education were at Eastern Boys' Government Primary school. Then he went on to St. Mary's College.

It was at that time, in 1970, an important turning point in the history of this country and globally, that Brian, like so many other young people began searching for answers.

This led him to take up the road of the people's striving to create a new world a world of freedom, not merely in words; a world where man can live in dignity and begin to make his story.

The path of devotion of the cause of the ordinary man is the road Brian traversed from then on.His student days from that point on took on a different

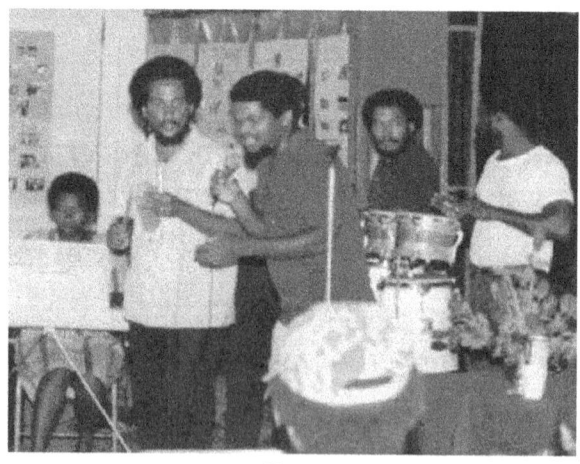

flavour from the familiar, yet he pursued healthy interests shared with most youth of his time.

The friendships he nurtured in his new Cascade community and at school persisted largely for the rest of his life.

After he left school, he became a worker on the Port of Port of Spain. He joined the workers' struggle and was active in a group that published a paper called "The Dockworkers' Bell" named after that bell that was the clarion call to action every time it was rung up and down the port.

After he became a school librarian, he remained an active member of his union.

Interest in Sports

Brian was an avid sportsman and unrepentant supporter of the soccer maestros of Brasil.

Rivelino, Jaizino, Pele, were his heroes and mentors.

In Cascade, Brian was an active member of Soul City football team where he earned even more nicknames, some resembling those of his heroes.

Incidentally, that is where Sir 13 first appeared and never disappeared.

Later, he became manager, coach, chief-cook-and-bottle-washer of Soul City Netball team. The court on which they practiced is now mired in controversy located as it is on the President's grounds, St. Anns.

Brian was a vociferous supporter of the West Indies cricket team and even made a robber hat to prove it.

Understanding that sports and politics could not be separated in 1986 Brian joined the protests against the South African tour of the West Indies outside the Oval in Port of Spain.

Hanging from a light pole on the day the police were ordered to try and smash that popular protest was a bobolee one of Brian's favourite artistic means of expression of his political views at that time.

For as long as his health permitted Brian actively participated in sport and worked tirelessly in the service of his beloved Soul City netball club.

Becoming the Artiste

At high school Brian first flirted with many of the talents for which he became so well-known and respected later.

He tried his hand at calypso composition and performance.

His lyrics always reflected his very serious concern for the plight of the poor and oppressed everywhere.

In the latter half of the 70's, his knack for producing biting lyrics emerged in a series of songs he composed and sang as Commentor.

One of them *Thousands More to Come* has grown into a virtual classic of the kai so of modem times.

It began:

> "I hear they want to hang Kirkland Paul and Michael Lewis
>
> for taking up arms against the imperialists;
>
> And they believe that repression
>
> Could hold back this great revolution;
>
> Tell them for me,
>
> They are surely wrong.
>
> They don't know
>
> They can't see
>
> That my people born to be free.
>
> Thousands more to come
>
> The struggle eh done
>
> Thousands more, thousands more
>
> Fighters for liberation"

This song was later part of the soundtrack of another of Brian's multifaceted cultural journey.

Throughout the 70's and from that time, Brian was a regular figure at strike camps, picket lines and everywhere that people were engaged in actions to secure their rights.

He composed several calypsos and chants.

In 1979 he was a founding member of the People's Cultural Association (PCA) and those performances in support of the various struggles of the people were as part of the performing group, an aspect of the Association's work.

Eventually, Brian became the Chairman of the PCA.

While participating in an International Sports and Cultural Festival in Britain as part of a PCA contingent, Brian wrote Divide and Rule, a powerful song against racism and anti-people violence.

Starting in 1981, Commentor made a series of recordings, the first Organised Nazi Rule a clarion call for a campaign against a political party the initials of which are easily recognised from its title.

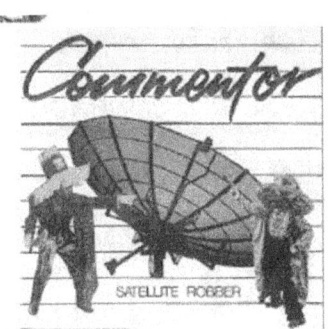

SATELLITE ROBBER

Later, two albums were recorded - "Satellite Robber•" and "Dragonslayer".

The first featured a very enlightening exchange of Robber talk with Andrew 'Puggy' Joseph.

The second featured several of Brian's compositions including "Heroes Carnival", "Blood Money" and a tribute to Frankie Francis.

The quality of Brian's calypsoes was reflected in the fact that he was included in the Calypso Monarch Semi-finals at least once.

For five years, as part of the PCA Brian was involved in producing a children's band. Its portrayals focused on traditional Carnival mas and educating the players on various aspects of the Carnival history.

So though mainly involved in the Kaiso arena, Brian dabbled in mas and other cultural work; not for the first time.

Transformation to O'Cangaceiro

The Brian most people know and remember is the man who played the robber mas.

In fact, Brian played robber period; not just mas.

Exploring creative ways to infuse this traditional cultural expression with new content became a mission and passion for Brian.

His first flirting with the Midnight Robber was in the field of calypso (kaiso as he preferred to call it).

In 1981, in seeking out an appropriate way in which to approach the subject of corruption in high places, Brian then as Commentor his calypso sobriquet penned and performed a piece called "Opera of the Midnight Robber ".

Using the imagery of Minshall's King of the band the previous year, he chose the idiom of robber talk to express his views.

It went like this:

> Stop! Stop, stop you mocking pretender
>
> Get down from my throne
>
> Peter Minshall Dat Midnight Robber was
>
> only a mass of bone
>
> When he come out to kill or slay
>
> He got to point revolver at men
>
> But when dis robber come to plunder

All he need is a ballpoint pen

Ent pulling off no robbery

risking shoot-out with Randy B

When I could open ah agency

for ah aeroplane company

Tell Minshall Gih meh back meh crown

Gih meh back meh crown

Gih meh back meh crown

I am de king robber in dis town

Tell him ah say ah w ant back inch crown.

Thus, was born, the Reincarnation of O'Cangaceiro, a character through which Brian developed the respected oral traditions of this special creation of the Trinidad Carnival, as an extension of the oral artistry of Africa in this Carnival cauldron.

Brian researched this art form and championed new views on its origins and infused it with new content, turning robber speech from bandit bravado to social commentary which had no season.

As recounted by Brian himself in a television special that has been aired every Carnival since its recording, his evolution into O'Cangaceiro, the most notorious bandido of the Brasilian sertao, began in 1981.

That year at Burrokeets Robber Talk competition in Belmont, he met Mr. Robber - Andrew 'Puggy' Joseph, the Agent of Death Valley.

The Agent invited O'Cangaceiro to join his band of merry marauders the following Carnival.

Dutifully, he met the master of the art by the Samaan tree at the Eastern entrance to the Savannah at the appointed time on Carnival Monday afternoon.

After some hesitation, as Brian tells it, he asked Puggy "Where is the rest of the band?"

To this, the reply came "This is the band!"

From that year the two and eventually more met at that same tree on both Carnival days annually. It remains the meeting place for the robbers of the Mystery Raiders, the band which Brian led till 2005.

After Puggy departed the city streets of the Carnival land in 1997,

Brian continued his mission to propel the Robber to new achievements.

Brian said, "My inspiration remains Andrew 'Puggy' Joseph."

He credited Puggy with showing him the possibilities of robber talk as poetry and social commentary.

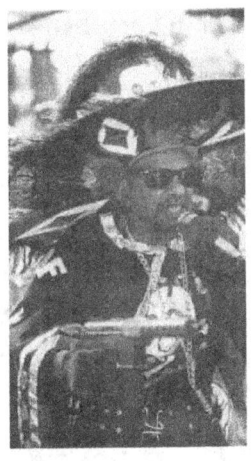 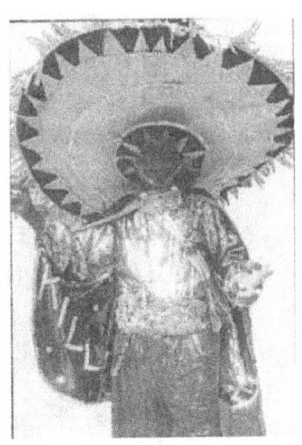

Andrew 'Puggy' Joseph   **Esau Millington**

The fact that Fuggy bequeathed his beloved Robber hat to Brian was an immense source of inspiration for him to continue to walk the road.

In 2006, the Mystery Raiders will roam the streets of the Carnival now led by the Melloncolly Marauder Anthony Collymore a close collaborator with Brian as a member of the band.

Exploring his Acting Talents

At a gathering at Brian's home in 2005, one of his Cascade friends commented that people seeing him portray certain characters in the plays with which he had found such enthusiasm would think he was acting well.

"But what they don't know" he continued, "is that Brian wasn't really acting. He was just being himself".

Such was his passion, his ability to identify with and internalise the characters he portrayed.

Talent was there, but more there was the passion.

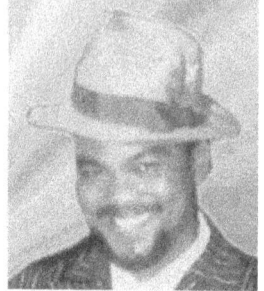

Posthumously, he was awarded the Cacique Award as Most Outstanding Actor for his role as Charlie in the 2004 production of **Moon on a Rainbow Shawl.**

Previously, Brian had been nominated in the same category going back to his role as King in **Lear Anansi***.*

His acting blossomed in the post-2000 period with consistently impressive performances in Elma **Francois: The Fire Inside** *as Butler and in* **An Echo in the Bone** *as well as in the two plays previously mentioned.*

Brian will be remembered for his music as well as his stage performances in three productions tracing the development of the calypso in the last century **Sing De Chorus, Ah Wanna Fall** *and* **The Roaring Seventies.**

Like his efforts in every other aspect of culture, Brian's acting was distinguished by his attention to detail and being faithful to history.

What kind of Man was this?

He has been called many things man of culture, of tradition and more by friend and foe alike. He was all of that and more.

He was at once a man of science and art, of tradition and about forging the new, about loving history and making it at the same time.

Both in his profession as a librarian and as a cultural activist, Brian paid attention to educating the next generation on the importance of the people's cultural traditions.

He was a fine example of the New Man the man of the future marching forward on the high road of civilisation.

One thing is certain Brian's unwavering devotion to the cause of the poor and dispossessed - the salt of the earth - will always characterise this brave champion of the people's culture.

O'Cangaceiro's Last Speech –

Saga of George Bushmaster[4]

Good evening, Mister Bushmaster

The street you are looking at is Marli Street, which belongs to the people of Trinbago ... a twin-island Republic off the coast of Venezuela.

This street has become important due to our international interests and hegemonic hysteria,

Your mission, should you decide to accept, is to steal this street ... and to convince the carnival audience that it has not been stolen.

Your disguise has been approved...

We suggest that you utilise a quaint literary device mastered by local politicians to fool the people ... namely The Robber Speech.

Should you be caught with your robber pants down,

This Carnival audience will disavow all knowledge of your sanity...

---

[4] *A satirical robber speech on the exploits of George Bush*

I am the voice of King George, Bushmaster, midnight robber, nuclear invader and street stealer!

From the day Satan gave birth to me

The doctor slapped me on my nuclear arsenal and declared that I will be commander-in-thief of the greatest superpower midnight robber army of this or any century.

At the age of one I declared that I alone must have the weapons of mass destruction monopoly

At the age of two, with my ancestor Custer, I slew Sitting Bull, Crazy Horse, Red Cloud and Geronimo confining their descendants to the reservation and gambling casino!

At the age of three I graduated from the Watergate University with a PhD in international propaganda and deceit.

I am also a member of the skill and cross bone society Dedicating my life to the destruction of Arafat, Saddam, Gaddafi, Chavez and Fidel as well.

Cuba watch out! You're next!

The game is over!

At the age of four I broke down the United Nations door Demanding a resolution to legitimise my war of annihilation While using

*my veto power to deny Palestine a homeland!
In 1945 it was Germany, Hiroshima and
Nagasaki.*

Guatemala, Panama twice in one century,

*Libya, Vietnam, Laos, Cambodia; Grenada in
1983 ... you name the country ... I invade it
already!*

*Our spy satellites have recently discovered
that you Trinbagonians have been developing
weapons of mass destruction in the Queen's
Park Savannah!*

A definite risk to our Marli Street minions!

*The first weapon: The National Carnival
Courthouse and Commess aka NCC*

*The second weapon is a misguided missile
named pan misguided because one week pan
coming from the West, next week pan corning
from the East*

*The third weapon of Mas[I] destruction: That
National Carnival Bikini and Beads
Association*

led by a terrorist more deadly than Osama!

"Barbarossa Bin Tiefin"

So you see

Marli Street is mine...

The road is mine...

The road is mine...

... this megalomaniac will self destruct in five seconds ...

Yuh oilfield or yuh life!

BRIAN HONORE

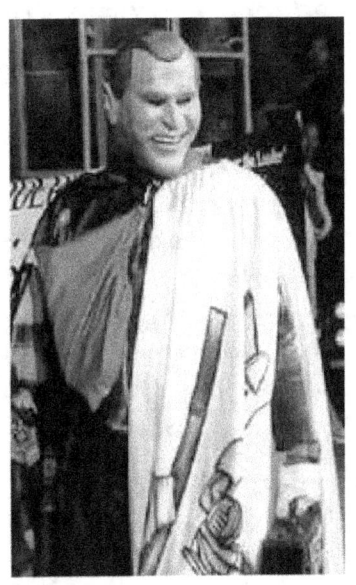

Farewell to Brian 'O'Cangaceiro' Honore

*A Tribute by Anthony Collymore, aka
The Melloncolly Marauder, now
Leader of the Mystery Raiders.*

Ole O'Cangaceiro, the most devious bandido to ever cross the Brazilian sertao!

Ole George Bushmaster, King George ruler of the western world, the dark and mysterious regions of the East. The heightless mountains of the Himalayas, the Valley of Desolation and the Hill of Forgotten men.

You perambulated the four corners of the Earth, crossed the Seven Seas, mighty oceans of despair and ignorance, bringing your messages of hope and education to every tortured soul and mocking-pretender you met.

Tirelessly you prowled the city streets, by night and by day, seeking to enlighten and uplift everyone fortunate enough to hear the thunderous words you had to say.

At the age of one your life's journey had just begun.

At the age of two your toys were canons and machine guns.

At the age of three you already had a vision of how the world should be.

You fought many an epic battle with sloth and ignorance, slaying many of their henchmen along the way. You slew the great dragon called Hydrophobia and turned the mighty Sahara Ocean into the desolate desert it still is today.

Four hundred years ago, your grandfather's treasures were stolen, in the heart of Africa, and you and many others were pitched forth on this distant shore. It was from that moment that you put on your Robber clothes to fight against the evil heritage of colonialism and cultural saturation.

You rubbed shoulders with Kings, yet never lost the common touch. Now the dragon don't walk these trails no more, the dragon don't walk these trails no more ,.. your shadow no longer darkens the Brazilian sertao, but your words will live on in the generations to follow.

No longer do you live on top the hill of Forgotten men, but now you are forever locked in the hearts of Men. You perambulate now on streets of gold, all your grandfather's treasures to behold.

Ole O'Cangaceiro, friend, teacher, role model, brother. Ole George-Bushmaster conqueror of the dreaded monsters of ignorance and cultural sterility. Your blood, sweat and tears will bear fruit in time to come ... Go, rest in peace, my brother, walk now with angels and fear not, the work of the Mystery Raiders is not yet done!

It is getting late, it is getting late, and you must present yourself at your Father's gate.

Fare thee well O'Cangaceiro, write your speeches now with the Golden Pen, and inspire us with your dreams from that distant shore, over yonder.

So speaketh The Melloncolly Marauder, on behalf of all the Mystery Raiders here present, those all over the world, the Universe, and many other places.

Veni, Vidi, Vici

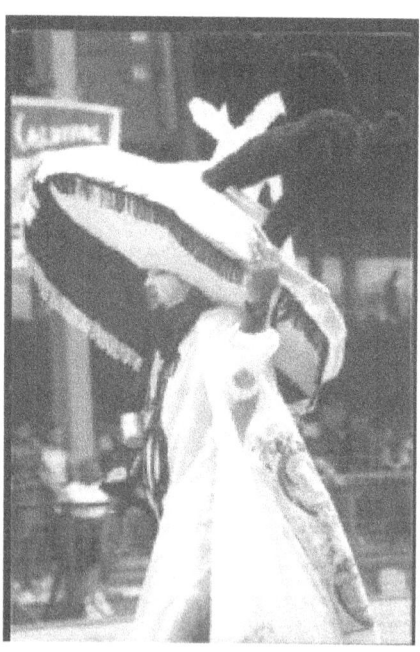

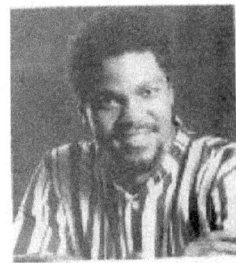

Brian Anthony Honore - *A man of the people, a cultural activist, calypsonian, robber man, actor, composer.*

Brian, born on 21 July 1955, was a patriotic artist whose contributions to the rich treasury of the people's culture of Trinidad and Tobago will long be remembered.

He was best known for his innovative work of introducing modern content to the oratory and art of the Midnight Robber, a traditional Carnival character.

Brian has left a great legacy of written and recorded calypso lyrics, robber speeches, costumes, memorable performances on stage and in the heart of the struggles of the workers and people.

The People's Cultural Association salutes the magnificent contribution of this outstanding fighter for the people's culture to the glorious cultural traditions of our people.

Bibliography

Anthony, Michael, *The Carnivals of Trinidad and Tobago – From Inception to Year 2000*, Port of Spain, Lonsdale Saatchi & Saatchi Ltd, 2011

Ashby, Muricia, *An Interview with mas man Ernest Thompson (Interviews with Famous Trinidadians Book 7)*, Kindle Edition, Muricia Ashby, 2013, ASIN: B00AYPD58U

Constance, Zeno Obi, *The Man Behind the Music: The People's Calypsonian*, Port of Spain, Zeno Obi Constance, 2010

Constance, Zeno Obi, *The Man and His Music – The Calypso lyrics of Bro. Valentino, The People's Calypsonian*, Port of Spain, Zeno Constance, 2017

George, Darcel Sashaleigh, *The Business of Bacchanal: how can Trinidad and Tobago develop its Carnival Industry as a viable export product and developmental tool ?*, Kindle Edition, Darcel George, 2018, ASIN: B07CSL84J3

Henry, Jeff, *Under the Mas': Resistance and Rebellion in the Trinidad Masquerade*, Port of Spain, Lexicon Trinidad Ltd, 2008

Hill, Errol, *The Trinidad Carnival: Mandate for a National Theatre*, Texas, University of Texas Press, 1972

Liverpool, Hollis "Chalkdust" Ph.D., *Rituals of Power and Rebellion – The Carnival Tradition in Trinidad & Tobago*

1763 - 1962, Chicago, Research Associates School Times Publications, 2001

Maharaj, George D., *The Roots of Calypso, Vols 1 &2,* Toronto, George Maharaj, 2001, 2005

Neil, Ancil Anthony, *Voices From the Hills – Despers & Laventille,* Port of Spain, Ancil Anthony Neil, 1987

Phillips, Everard M., *The Political Calypso: A Sociolinguistic Process of Conflict Transformation,* Port of Spain, Everard Phillips, 2009

Trinidad Carnival – A Republication of Caribbean Quarterly 1956, Port of Spain, Paria Publishing Co. Ltd, 1988

Quevedo, Raymond "Atilla", *Atilla's Kaiso – A Short History of Trinidad Calypso,* St. Augustine, University of the West Indies, 1983, 1994

www.ingramcontent.com/pod-product-compliance
Lightning Source LLC
Chambersburg PA
CBHW071236220526
45468CB00002B/883